Simply the Word

Word

(Book 3)

Heavenly Word Waters

Bishop Gregory Leacham

To the PASTOR from the BISHOP Blessing ARE Here for You.

First Printing

Revival Waves of Glory Books & Publishing has allowed this work to remain exactly as the author intended, verbatim, without editorial input.

All Scripture quotations are from the Authorized King James Version of the Bible.

EBook 978-1-312-52295-4
Softcover 978-1-312-52291-6
Hardcover 978-1-312-52292-3

PUBLISHED BY REVIVAL WAVES OF GLORY
BOOKS & PUBLISHING
www.revivalwavesofgloryministries.com
Litchfield, IL

Printed in the United States of America

Table of Contents

Bishop Gregory Leacham is a

prophetic writer and inspired by the

Holy Spirit.

Introduction

I came from no where to His somewhere in Him, Him who my Jesus, When He really looked into my Life, with my Heart wide open For His Help, everything changed, my mind, Heart, body & soul. Then I knew purpose, His for my Life was needed.

What Jesus did to me, no other man or woman or money or false power could ever do. He gave ME and filled ME with His wisdom to help others. However, I have learned from Jesus. You must learn how to except it his right, Jesus hates pride. The bible says that we are forever learning, but are we able to come to the knowledge of Jesus' truth.

Except that, you come as a child humble pie. The world of God, eat good.

This book was written with you in heart

Not Today Tomorrow

Who knows the seen and unseen better than Jesus, He see's what's right in front of you, when you don't He see's what's behind you when, you can't He sees what's ahead of you when you're blind or blinded by what you have or think you have, not today tomorrow wait for it, it's better when it's God ready for you. Don't know yet. Have you not learn?

This holy race is not given to the swift or to the strong, but to them that endure to the end of their flesh, to gain spiritual strength, to be seated wit Jesus for-ever so hurry up and take your right time to die to what you think you know, remember you must lose to gain, not today, tomorrow Jesus already set his time for you, hear his voice.

Word helpers:

Psalms 95:7-11 For he *is* our God; and we *are* the people of his pasture, and the sheep of his hand. To day if ye will hear his voice, Harden not your heart, as in the provocation, *and* as *in* the day of temptation in the wilderness: When your fathers tempted me, proved me, and saw my work. Forty years long was I grieved with *this* generation, and said, It *is* a people that do err in their heart, and they have not known my ways: Unto whom I sware in my wrath that they should not enter into my rest.

Hebrews 3:7-11 Wherefore (as the Holy Ghost saith, To day if ye will hear his voice, Harden not your hearts, as in the provocation, in the day of temptation in the wilderness: When your fathers tempted me, proved me, and saw my works forty years. Wherefore I was grieved with that generation, and said, They do alway err in *their* heart; and they have not known my ways. So I sware in my wrath, They shall not enter into my rest.)

Catch the Fire

This is the Fire that burns, but does not consume you it burns up what's not like Christ in you it burns up your old ways your evil ways your wicked ways your wicked thoughts that leads you into doing evil deeds. The fire gets to the root of your bondage and burns it upward from the inside out, so Jesus can put in more of him, Jesus said I will not and cannot dwell in an unclean temple. So here comes the fire, the burning up from the inside out fire, the new heart fire, the mind of Christ fire, the living holy fire , the focus on Jesus fire, the no more I, I, I or me, me, me, fire just yes Lord. Amen

Living holy fire:

> Matthew 3:11-12 I indeed baptize you with water unto repentance: but he that cometh after me is mightier than I, whose shoes I am not worthy to bear: he shall baptize you with the Holy Ghost, and *with* fire: Whose fan *is* in his hand, and he will throughly purge his floor, and gather his wheat into the garner; but he will burn up the chaff with unquenchable fire.

Holy fire, correction:

> Deuteronomy 5:4-9 The LORD talked with you face to face in the mount out of the midst of the fire, (I stood between the LORD and you at that time, to shew you the word of the LORD: for ye were afraid by reason of the fire, and went not up into the mount;) saying, I *am* the LORD thy God, which brought thee out of the land of Egypt, from the house of bondage. Thou shalt have none other gods before me. Thou shalt not make thee *any* graven

11

image, *or* any likeness *of any thing* that *is* in heaven above, or that *is* in the earth beneath, or that *is* in the waters beneath the earth: Thou shalt not bow down thyself unto them, nor serve them: for I the LORD thy God *am* a jealous God, visiting the iniquity of the fathers upon the children unto the third and fourth *generation* of them that hate me,

Deuteronomy 4:24-27 For the LORD thy God *is* a consuming fire, *even* a jealous God. When thou shalt beget children, and children's children, and ye shall have remained long in the land, and shall corrupt *yourselves,* and make a graven image, *or* the likeness of any *thing,* and shall do evil in the sight of the LORD thy God, to provoke him to anger: I call heaven and earth to witness against you this day, that ye shall soon utterly perish from off the land whereunto ye go over Jordan to possess it; ye shall not prolong *your* days upon it, but shall utterly be destroyed. And the LORD shall scatter you among the nations, and ye shall be left few in number among the heathen, whither the LORD shall lead you.

Holy fire:

Hebrews 1:7 And of the angels he saith, Who maketh his angels spirits, and his ministers a flame of fire.

Luke 12:49 I am come to send fire on the earth; and what will I, if it be already kindled?

1 Corinthians 3:10-17 According to the grace of God which is given unto me, as a wise masterbuilder, I have laid the foundation, and another buildeth thereon. But let every man take heed how he buildeth thereupon. For other foundation can no man lay than that is laid, which is Jesus Christ. Now if any man build upon this

foundation gold, silver, precious stones, wood, hay, stubble; Every man's work shall be made manifest: for the day shall declare it, because it shall be revealed by fire; and the fire shall try every man's work of what sort it is. If any man's work abide which he hath built thereupon, he shall receive a reward. If any man's work shall be burned, he shall suffer loss: but he himself shall be saved; yet so as by fire. Know ye not that ye are the temple of God, and *that* the Spirit of God dwelleth in you? If any man defile the temple of God, him shall God destroy; for the temple of God is holy, which *temple* ye are.

Deuteronomy 4:12-20 And the LORD spake unto you out of the midst of the fire: ye heard the voice of the words, but saw no similitude; only *ye heard* a voice. And he declared unto you his covenant, which he commanded you to perform, *even* ten commandments; and he wrote them upon two tables of stone. And the LORD commanded me at that time to teach you statutes and judgments, that ye might do them in the land whither ye go over to possess it. Take ye therefore good heed unto yourselves; for ye saw no manner of similitude on the day *that* the LORD spake unto you in Horeb out of the midst of the fire: Lest ye corrupt *yourselves,* and make you a graven image, the similitude of any figure, the likeness of male or female, The likeness of any beast that *is* on the earth, the likeness of any winged fowl that flieth in the air, The likeness of any thing that creepeth on the ground, the likeness of any fish that *is* in the waters beneath the earth: And lest thou lift up thine eyes unto heaven, and when thou seest the sun, and the moon, and the stars, *even* all the host of heaven, shouldest be driven to worship them, and serve them, which the LORD thy God hath divided unto all nations under the whole heaven. But the LORD hath taken you, and brought you forth out of the iron furnace, *even* out of Egypt, to be unto him a people of inheritance, as *ye are* this day.

Simply the Word

All or Nothing
Withholding Nothing

Main meat:

> Mark 10:46-52 And they came to Jericho: and as he went out of Jericho with his disciples and a great number of people, blind Bartimaeus, the son of Timaeus, sat by the highway side begging. And when he heard that it was Jesus of Nazareth, he began to cry out, and say, Jesus, *thou* Son of David, have mercy on me. And many charged him that he should hold his peace: but he cried the more a great deal, *Thou* Son of David, have mercy on me. And Jesus stood still, and commanded him to be called. And they call the blind man, saying unto him, Be of good comfort, rise; he calleth thee. And he, casting away his garment, rose, and came to Jesus. And Jesus answered and said unto him, What wilt thou that I should do unto thee? The blind man said unto him, Lord, that I might receive my sight. And Jesus said unto him, Go thy way; thy faith hath made thee whole. And immediately he received his sight, and followed Jesus in the way.

Focus Verse:

> Psalms 19:6-14 His going forth *is* from the end of the heaven, and his circuit unto the ends of it: and there is nothing hid from the heat thereof. The law of the LORD *is* perfect, converting the soul: the testimony of the LORD *is* sure, making wise the simple. The statutes of the LORD *are* right, rejoicing the heart: the commandment of the LORD *is* pure, enlightening the eyes. The fear of the LORD *is* clean, enduring for ever: the judgments of the LORD *are* true *and* righteous altogether. More to be desired *are they* than gold, yea, than much fine

15

gold: sweeter also than honey and the honeycomb. Moreover by them is thy servant warned: *and* in keeping of them *there is* great reward. Who can understand *his* errors? cleanse thou me from secret *faults.* Keep back thy servant also from presumptuous *sins;* let them not have dominion over me: then shall I be upright, and I shall be innocent from the great transgression. Let the words of my mouth, and the meditation of my heart, be acceptable in thy sight, O LORD, my strength, and my redeemer.

Take these three easy steps.

1. Admit that you are withholding something and you need Jesus to release you from it.

2. Follow the God given instructions to be set free, and learn how to stay free.

3. Learn how to stay away from your bondage

Help tips

Lord teach me and help me to search myself daily, and to confess and repeat to you daily, so I can give you all and withholding nothing, teach me Lord I cry out from my heart. I surrender what I think I know, for the one who knows everything.

Word helpers – old nothing, new all 2 Corinthians 5:17, Matthew 21:18-19 Jesus went to the fig tree and found nothing , not of you can be found, it has to be Jesus fruit found in you from now on.

The more people who need Jesus the better
Matthew 20:29-34

Simply the Word

Jesus Is Ready to Take Your Order, Are You Ready to Put the Right One In?

Orders Jesus is Looking For

1. Try his new way everyday – Jesus the same today, yesterday and forever
2. Avoid the line – Joshua 24:15
3. Order on his one way on line help – Matthew 4:4
4. Order now for your rapid pick up plan of salvation – Matthew 7:13-14
5. Order from his unfailing history of saving souls – Acts 4:1-13
6. Save your customized place with him in heaven, he that endures to the END the same shall be saved.
7. Enter for your life time credit card once and for all – 1 Corinthians 6:20, 1 Corinthians 7:22-24
8. Don't delay your pick up time – Hell is waiting

Help tips for putting in the right order

1. Get under the right order, the God given leader, to and for you and follow him as he or she follows Christ – Jeremiah 3:15

2. Learn how to die to your fleshly lust – Philippians 1:21

3. You will seek me and find me, when (You) have seeked me with your whole heart – Psalms 63:1, Psalms 119:1-11, Jeremiah 29:10-14

Three main reasons why we don't seek God right

1. Fear
2. Double Minded
3. Or you just don't care

My Mind Is Anchored In the Lord

Ephesians 4:23 And be renewed in the spirit of your mind;

Romans 6:1-2 What shall we say then? Shall we continue in sin, that grace may abound? God forbid. How shall we, that are dead to sin, live any longer therein?

Romans 6:22-23 But now being made free from sin, and become servants to God, ye have your fruit unto holiness, and the end everlasting life. For the wages of sin *is* death; but the gift of God *is* eternal life through Jesus Christ our Lord.

My mind is anchored in the Lord
My things
My thoughts
My desires
My emotions
My feelings
My heart
My right
My wrong
My soul
My being corrected, through his word, daily when he says it's enough

Romans 7:19-23 For the good that I would I do not: but the evil which I would not, that I do. Now if I do that I would not, it is no more I that do it, but sin that dwelleth in me. I find then a law, that, when I would do good, evil is present with me. For I delight in the law of God after the inward man: But I see another law in my members, warring against the law of my mind, and bringing me into captivity to the law of sin which is in my members.

Every time I want or go to do good, evil is always present, to help me to go in it's way choice given, choice made

Romans 6:16 – you choose

Romans 6:14 – Jesus freed you

Choose this each and everyday when you will serve. Before you leave your home, you do anyway

The loaded spirit

John 3:1-12 Meat to Eat

A religious person can tell you something but they can't tell you have the right way to do it. You must have a born-again into Jesus relationship. Then you can show and tell, it's not what you say that directs people right, it's what you live. Because what you say really shows how and who you believe in and serve. Don't drop that loaded gun it might go off and hurt someone. That's the same thing when you keep your loaded dead spirit. Jesus said let the dead bury and dead. Jesus said your wisdom is foolishness to him, will you instruct God. God forbid it is better to obey God rather than man get a Jesus relationship for your self.

Loaded means
Ready to explode, ready to let loose, ready to go, ready to move, ready to start, ready to jump on full, full of what, full of who? Don't care just do it? Ready to let someone have it, what I think is right and wrong, can't wait, can't see right ready to leap, before I look Jesus said if you don't do this - John 3:3 You will never know me right, my right. Amen

Simply the Word

Get Lost In Jesus, Then You Will Be Twice Dead Right

John 3:6-12 That which is born of the flesh is flesh; and that which is born of the Spirit is spirit. Marvel not that I said unto thee, Ye must be born again. The wind bloweth where it listeth, and thou hearest the sound thereof, but canst not tell whence it cometh, and whither it goeth: so is every one that is born of the Spirit. Nicodemus answered and said unto him, How can these things be? Jesus answered and said unto him, Art thou a master of Israel, and knowest not these things? Verily, verily, I say unto thee, We speak that we do know, and testify that we have seen; and ye receive not our witness. If I have told you earthly things, and ye believe not, how shall ye believe, if I tell you *of* heavenly things?

2 Corinthians 12:1-6 It is not expedient for me doubtless to glory. I will come to visions and revelations of the Lord. I knew a man in Christ above fourteen years ago, (whether in the body, I cannot tell; or whether out of the body, I cannot tell: God knoweth;) such an one caught up to the third heaven. And I knew such a man, (whether in the body, or out of the body, I cannot tell: God knoweth;) How that he was caught up into paradise, and heard unspeakable words, which it is not lawful for a man to utter. Of such an one will I glory: yet of myself I will not glory, but in mine infirmities. For though I would desire to glory, I shall not be a fool; for I will say the truth: but *now* I forbear, lest any man should think of me above that which he seeth me *to be,* or *that* he heareth of me.

Word Helpers – Colossians 2:20-23, Romans 6:11, Romans 6:7, 1 Peter 2:24, 1 Thessalonians 4:16

Dead in Christ	Dead without Christ
Dead for his use	Dead to his use
Made something for his good	Made for a fool's good Death

Life	Death
Learn right	Learn wrong
Spirit filled	Flesh filled
Seeing Me	Living in
Light	Darkness
Doing all	Limited
Things through	In my flesh
Christ	Knowledge

Lord teach me how to lose my mind and gain the mind of Christ Jesus, then I can get lost in Jesus and be dead right, your right. Amen

Jesus Said, This Is What You Live By

Genesis 1:1 In the beginning God created the heaven and the earth.

John 15:21-25 But all these things will they do unto you for my name's sake, because they know not him that sent me. If I had not come and spoken unto them, they had not had sin: but now they have no cloke for their sin. He that hateth me hateth my Father also. If I had not done among them the works which none other man did, they had not had sin: but now have they both seen and hated both me and my Father. But *this cometh to pass,* that the word might be fulfilled that is written in their law, They hated me without a cause.

1 John 1:1-10 That which was from the beginning, which we have heard, which we have seen with our eyes, which we have looked upon, and our hands have handled, of the Word of life; (For the life was manifested, and we have seen *it,* and bear witness, and shew unto you that eternal life, which was with the Father, and was manifested unto us;) That which we have seen and heard declare we unto you, that ye also may have fellowship with us: and truly our fellowship *is* with the Father, and with his Son Jesus Christ. And these things write we unto you, that your joy may be full. This then is the message which we have heard of him, and declare unto you, that God is light, and in him is no darkness at all. If we say that we have fellowship with him, and walk in darkness, we lie, and do not the truth: But if we walk in the light, as he is in the light, we have fellowship one with another, and the blood of Jesus

Christ his Son cleanseth us from all sin. If we say that we have no sin, we deceive ourselves, and the truth is not in us. If we confess our sins, he is faithful and just to forgive us *our* sins, and to cleanse us from all unrighteousness. If we say that we have not sinned, we make him a liar, and his word is not in us.

1 John 2:1-11 My little children, these things write I unto you, that ye sin not. And if any man sin, we have an advocate with the Father, Jesus Christ the righteous: And he is the propitiation for our sins: and not for ours only, but also for *the sins of* the whole world. And hereby we do know that we know him, if we keep his commandments. He that saith, I know him, and keepeth not his commandments, is a liar, and the truth is not in him. But whoso keepeth his word, in him verily is the love of God perfected: hereby know we that we are in him. He that saith he abideth in him ought himself also so to walk, even as he walked. Brethren, I write no new commandment unto you, but an old commandment which ye had from the beginning. The old commandment is the word which ye have heard from the beginning. Again, a new commandment I write unto you, which thing is true in him and in you: because the darkness is past, and the true light now shineth. He that saith he is in the light, and hateth his brother, is in darkness even until now. He that loveth his brother abideth in the light, and there is none occasion of stumbling in him. But he that hateth his brother is in darkness, and walketh in darkness, and knoweth not whither he goeth, because that darkness hath blinded his eyes.

1. Genesis 1:26 – who is us?

Father Genesis 1:1 in creation, SON Colossians 1:12-15 son in redemption, Holy Ghost Act 2:1-4 Holy Ghost in dwelling spirit.

2. What I did already – John 15:3-4
3. John 3:3 – John 3:5-8 – John 14:25-27
What I did already

I have set my people in place for all of you, from the beginning , to help and correct you, think back, it just didn't start at home or in school, it's everywhere you go, obey those who have rule over you, I the Lord your God set them in place for you, known or unknown to you. Stop your fight, learn to take heed, time is short very for you. Listen and learn

Jesus said this is what you live by

You don't know, if you don't really know me. If you always say I know, I know, that's pride. Just say thank you.

My knowing is doing it right, your right will fall apart, like vapor. Learn to live by me.

In Me, you have life only.

Jesus said – Live by

By every word of mind that comes forth out of my mouth and those who I have sent to you, to her and do. You know when I send them; my truth will always stick on you. With Holy Ghost glue. The best glue every made. Amen

Simply the Word

Leadership, How Do I Know If They Are Following Christ?

John 3:28-30 Ye yourselves bear me witness, that I said, I am not the Christ, but that I am sent before him. He that hath the bride is the bridegroom: but the friend of the bridegroom, which standeth and heareth him, rejoiceth greatly because of the bridegroom's voice: this my joy therefore is fulfilled. He must increase, but I *must* decrease.

1.   First, pray and ask the Lord Jesus to send you to the church he wants you at, the right leader is already there.

2.   Jeremiah 3:15, Jeremiah 3:6-14

If they are not helping to create a change in you with their own life style, look again

3.   If they are compromising with you all the time, look again

4.   If they won't tell you God's truth for your life, look again – Romans 8:14-17

5.   If you keep coming in the same way, you left out, time after time, you don't want it. Then they should tell you the truth about you, always watch, and see your affect on others. Misery Loves Company.

The Lord Said, What's the matter With Love?

The Lord said first, I am not in it. Your way, lust love, if you give me love, I love how you do it love, today and maybe I do. Tell them what they want to hear love.

I love all of my sex partner's love

What's love go to do with it? Sure I love you, don't I always say it.

I love you but I don't really have time to listen or spend with you.

There are other things that are more important, you see

The Lord said stop treating ME like a little dab-will-do-ya or you

I must have unconditional love or none

Your fake love stinks

What does love have to do with it? Everything

Only Jesus can love you fully and right. He gave his life for us all Did you?

> John 3:16-21 For God so loved the world, that he gave his only begotten Son, that whosoever believeth in him should not perish, but have everlasting life. For God sent not his Son into the world to condemn the world; but that the world through him might be saved. He that believeth on him is not condemned: but he that believeth not is

condemned already, because he hath not believed in the name of the only begotten Son of God. And this is the condemnation, that light is come into the world, and men loved darkness rather than light, because their deeds were evil. For every one that doeth evil hateth the light, neither cometh to the light, lest his deeds should be reproved. But he that doeth truth cometh to the light, that his deeds may be made manifest, that they are wrought in God.

The Wonder Bread – It Works Wonders All Over You

The Tempter Is Coming

Matthew 4:1-11 Then was Jesus led up of the Spirit into the wilderness to be tempted of the devil. And when he had fasted forty days and forty nights, he was afterward an hungred. And when the tempter came to him, he said, If thou be the Son of God, command that these stones be made bread. But he answered and said, It is written, Man shall not live by bread alone, but by every word that proceedeth out of the mouth of God. Then the devil taketh him up into the holy city, and setteth him on a pinnacle of the temple, And saith unto him, If thou be the Son of God, cast thyself down: for it is written, He shall give his angels charge concerning thee: and in *their* hands they shall bear thee up, lest at any time thou dash thy foot against a stone. Jesus said unto him, It is written again, Thou shalt not tempt the Lord thy God. Again, the devil taketh him up into an exceeding high mountain, and sheweth him all the kingdoms of the world, and the glory of them; And saith unto him, All these things will I give thee, if thou wilt fall down and worship me. Then saith Jesus unto him, Get thee hence, Satan: for it is written, Thou shalt worship the Lord thy God, and him only shalt thou serve. Then the devil leaveth him, and, behold, angels came and ministered unto him.

Focus Verse – Matthew 4:4 – Man shall not live by bread alone, but by every word that comes out of the mouth of God, written and rhema word, which is my spiritual revelation, that I give out.

Jesus said I am the bread of life; with Me on the outside of you won't work right. You can't look like me on the outside, until my bread gets down, down on the inside of you, to help you change and strengthen you.

Just like natural bread it doesn't do you any good just looking at it. You have to eat it in-order for it to help you. In-order for you to get the right strength and help from it you really need God created it for your purpose, not his.

This bread will run out, but Jesus the bread of life won't. Have you really tried him in his truth he cannot lie or die? Amen

The Gathering

Jesus Said Welcome To My Harvest, Yours Is Burning

Matthews 13:24-30 Another parable put he forth unto them, saying, The kingdom of heaven is likened unto a man which sowed good seed in his field: But while men slept, his enemy came and sowed tares among the wheat, and went his way. But when the blade was sprung up, and brought forth fruit, then appeared the tares also. So the servants of the householder came and said unto him, Sir, didst not thou sow good seed in thy field? from whence then hath it tares? He said unto them, An enemy hath done this. The servants said unto him, Wilt thou then that we go and gather them up? But he said, Nay; lest while ye gather up the tares, ye root up also the wheat with them. Let both grow together until the harvest: and in the time of harvest I will say to the reapers, Gather ye together first the tares, and bind them in bundles to burn them: but gather the wheat into my barn.

Jesus said, I will keep you, you will give yourself away – Matthew 13:36-43

Jesus said a lot of you have already made up in your hearts, that you really don't want this Jesus who you heard and hear about, you only want what's in his hand, Jesus said my true love for you are still waiting on you, and will you come?

Simply the Word

Jesus Changes Not!

Jesus Said He Dropped the Charges and Jesus Said I Changed the Verdict or SINtance and Sentence.

Jesus said what more could he do. He laid the foundation and open up the door.

Jesus has thrown it into the sea of forgiveness, but you can mess up, he won't thank you Jesus.

Walk by faith and not by sight

Jesus said he dropped the charges.

If I do, he will keep his appointment with me. If I do what?

Learn how to obey Jesus without compromise or complaining or trying to put our know nothing self in it or in his way

Word helpers – Genesis 18:1-15, Genesis 21:1-7

You came in this world with nothing, and but you can leave with heavenly salvation. Amen

Simply the Word

Who Is Producing You?

Genesis 1:28 And God blessed them, and God said unto them, Be fruitful, and multiply, and replenish the earth, and subdue it: and have dominion over the fish of the sea, and over the fowl of the air, and over every living thing that moveth upon the earth.

Every spirit reproduces after it's own spirit

Main meat – Genesis 1:1-27, as revealed by Jesus to me for you. Amen

Genesis 1:1 – God already knew who was going to stay in heaven on earth and who would stay under the earth in hell.

Genesis 1:2 – Then God divided his people of light, from the devil's people of darkness

Genesis 1:3 – Then he called his people light and the other people darkness, because they loved sin and love to serve it.

Genesis 1:4 – but God, being God and loving created a place for both of us, for a time to live in and get it his right.

Genesis 1:5 – and God said let everything reproduce after it's own kind

Genesis 1:6 – Then God said let's divide the pure water from the unpure waters, I know their hearts, I made them all in our image but, not all will be born-again for my use.

Genesis 1:7 – The Lord separated his people for heaven and evil one's people for hell from the beginning.

Genesis 1:8 – and God called his people heaven bound.

Genesis 1:9 – God said I will have mercy on all, give them a chance to be watered by me.

Genesis 1:10 – there are more of us than there are of them, open up your spiritual eye and see out of mine.

Genesis 1:11 – let everything be born-again of itself, like you must be born again of me my holy spirit to see and understand me right.

Genesis 1:12 – God made everything to reproduce after it's own kind, who's kind are you? God's good or your bad?

Genesis 1:13 – God has a set time.

Genesis 1:14 – God said my kind will always show my light and my ways a sign and for-ever.

Genesis 1:15 – Let my people be my example.

Genesis 1:16 – Some of my lights will do greater works and some lesser, then there are those who trust hang around.

Genesis 1:17 – Jesus said to much is given much is required

Genesis 1:18 – Jesus said I have leaders of light, and some that chose darkeness, I created good and evil for my purpose, and all things work out for my good

Genesis 1:20 – Jesus said let those who are full of my word, bring forth more souls

Genesis 1:21 – Jesus said I will make your name great and take you up after me.

Genesis 1:22 – Jesus said I approved you and blessed you, and said reproduce after me, spiritually and naturally.

Genesis 1:24-27 – Jesus said let us make all these living creatures after their own kind. But let us make man greater special, after our own image, after our own likeness, and let's give him dominion and rule over all other creation, that we made. Don't forget he man will need help or a help for meet a woman, a wife of my covenant or choice for them to last my right, made together by me, I and only I the Lord God, can take and put some of each of you in each other to make it my right. Amen

In the greatest book on earth, the bible in the book of Ecclesiastes 1:9 it say's there is nothing new under the son.

What was is now, I the Lord God knew the end from the beginning.

This is what you get when you chose to disobey the right producer.

> Genesis 2:9 And out of the ground made the LORD God to grow every tree that is pleasant to the sight, and good for food; the tree of life also in the midst of the garden, and the tree of knowledge of good and evil.

> Genesis 2:16-17 And the LORD God commanded the man, saying, Of every tree of the garden thou mayest freely eat: But of the tree of the knowledge of good and evil, thou shalt not eat of it: for in the day that thou eatest thereof thou shalt surely die.

> Genesis 3:1-3 Now the serpent was more subtil than any beast of the field which the LORD God had made. And he said unto the woman, Yea, hath God said, Ye shall not eat of every tree of the garden? And the woman said unto the serpent, We may eat of the fruit of the trees of the garden: But of the fruit of the tree which *is* in the midst of the garden, God hath said, Ye shall not eat of it, neither shall ye touch it, lest ye die.

> Genesis 3:4-12 And the serpent said unto the woman, Ye shall not surely die: For God doth know that in the day ye eat thereof, then your eyes shall be opened, and ye shall be as gods, knowing good and evil. And when the woman saw that the tree *was* good for food, and that it *was* pleasant to the eyes, and a tree to be desired to make *one* wise, she took of the fruit thereof, and did eat, and gave also unto her husband with her; and he did eat. And the eyes of them both were opened, and they knew that they *were* naked; and they sewed fig leaves together, and made themselves aprons. And they heard the voice of the LORD God walking in the garden in the cool of the day: and Adam and his

wife hid themselves from the presence of the LORD God amongst the trees of the garden. And the LORD God called unto Adam, and said unto him, Where *art* thou? And he said, I heard thy voice in the garden, and I was afraid, because I *was* naked; and I hid myself. And he said, Who told thee that thou *wast* naked? Hast thou eaten of the tree, whereof I commanded thee that thou shouldest not eat? And the man said, The woman whom thou gavest *to be* with me, she gave me of the tree, and I did eat.

The whole world is a stage and everybody play's their part.

God's good or of your father the devil's evil.

That's why you are and everybody will choose this everyday whom we will serve, before you leave your house or place of living.

The Lord said, that's why you must be born-again of me, to be reproduced to learn how to produce my right.

This is the listen to learn section

He who hath ears to hear, let him hear, what the spirit of the Lord say's to his church. Amen

Simply the Word

The Other Affair Cry Out for Help You Need Deliverance

Jesus said how many other spirits are you sleeping with? Or involved with, or shacking up with or under the wrong covenant with. Jesus said if you are not with me, you are against me. Him alone, not trying to serve two masters, you can-not.

Can you change you own spirit? NO. It takes the one and only true and living God. Slaves love to act like their masters. If you love what you are doing, you won't stop, until you are dead and in the wrong place for-ever it's called hell, who's your master?

Whose fool are you?

Unfaithfulness breaks the bond of trust the foundation of all relationships Jesus said without faith in him it is impossible to please him. He said he would bless the faithful and righteous and protect them as with a shield.

Who's covering you? The creator or the condemner?

Make the right choice. Amen

Real word helpers – Deuteronomy 8:3, Matthew 4:3-4

Simply the Word

What's Left?

Genesis 1:11-12 And God said, Let the earth bring forth grass, the herb yielding seed, *and* the fruit tree yielding fruit after his kind, whose seed *is* in itself, upon the earth: and it was so. And the earth brought forth grass, *and* herb yielding seed after his kind, and the tree yielding fruit, whose seed *was* in itself, after his kind: and God saw that *it was* good.

Genesis 1:21 And God created great whales, and every living creature that moveth, which the waters brought forth abundantly, after their kind, and every winged fowl after his kind: and God saw that *it was* good.

Genesis 1:24-25 And God said, Let the earth bring forth the living creature after his kind, cattle, and creeping thing, and beast of the earth after his kind: and it was so. And God made the beast of the earth after his kind, and cattle after their kind, and every thing that creepeth upon the earth after his kind: and God saw that *it was* good.

Genesis 1:31 And God saw every thing that he had made, and, behold, *it was* very good. And the evening and the morning were the sixth day.

Matthew 6:25-34 Therefore I say unto you, Take no thought for your life, what ye shall eat, or what ye shall drink; nor yet for your body, what ye shall put on. Is not the life more than meat, and the body than raiment? Behold the fowls of the air: for they sow not, neither do they reap, nor gather into barns; yet your heavenly Father feedeth them. Are ye not much better than they? Which of you by taking thought can add one cubit unto his stature? And why take ye thought for raiment? Consider the lilies of the field, how they grow; they toil not, neither do they spin: And yet I say unto you, That even Solomon in all his glory was not arrayed like one of these. Wherefore, if God so clothe the grass of the field, which to day is, and to morrow is cast into the oven, *shall he* not much more *clothe* you, O ye of little faith? Therefore take no thought, saying, What shall we eat? or, What shall we drink? or, Wherewithal shall we be clothed? (For after all these things do the Gentiles seek:) for your heavenly Father knoweth that ye have need of all these things. But seek ye first the kingdom of God, and his righteousness; and all these things shall be added unto you. Take therefore no thought for the morrow: for the morrow shall take thought for the things of itself. Sufficient unto the day *is* the evil thereof.

1. How much have you given out?
2. How much have you wasted?
3. How much have you thrown away?
4. How much will or has it cost you?
5. How much has it cost others in your life?
6. How could you have helped in what's left, to have more left?
7. What's left, what is it worth? Or who wants it anymore?
8. Maybe I need to let Jesus restore me all over-again, Born-me-again Jesus make me your real, and then I won't steal my life from you.

Simply the Word Nuggets From Heaven for You

Lord prepare ME, to be or not to be just for you, tear me down for you. Let me die for you, build me up for you. Lord blind me for you, correct me for you Lord shut me up for you, Lord make me for you, let me love for you, speak for you live holy for you, listen for you, Lord not for me, but for you, preaching and teaching for you, Lord le me see for you, Lord with you

Follow us, but who is telling you this?

1. What's your extreme want?
2. Who is driving you to it?
3. What outcome will you receive?
4. Will it hurt others?
5. Will it send you to hell?
6. Matthew 6:33

It's time – Ecclesiastes 3:1-2

1. It's time to do God's right and God's wrong according to the world's system
2. You think like who you run with
3. If you give money to people who are not use to having it, they will always spend it on something not good for them.

4. Some must die, so others will live, some must live, that others will die. There is God's set time for everything to come to pass under his authority.

Noise, Noise, Noise, Who's Noise Are You Living By?

Daniel 3:1-18 Nebuchadnezzar the king made an image of gold, whose height *was* threescore cubits, *and* the breadth thereof six cubits: he set it up in the plain of Dura, in the province of Babylon. Then Nebuchadnezzar the king sent to gather together the princes, the governors, and the captains, the judges, the treasurers, the counsellors, the sheriffs, and all the rulers of the provinces, to come to the dedication of the image which Nebuchadnezzar the king had set up. Then the princes, the governors, and captains, the judges, the treasurers, the counsellors, the sheriffs, and all the rulers of the provinces, were gathered together unto the dedication of the image that Nebuchadnezzar the king had set up; and they stood before the image that Nebuchadnezzar had set up. Then an herald cried aloud, To you it is commanded, O people, nations, and languages, *That* at what time ye hear the sound of the cornet, flute, harp, sackbut, psaltery, dulcimer, and all kinds of musick, ye fall down and worship the golden image that Nebuchadnezzar the king hath set up: And whoso falleth not down and worshippeth shall the same hour be cast into the midst of a burning fiery furnace. Therefore at that time, when all the people heard the sound of the cornet, flute, harp, sackbut, psaltery, and all kinds of musick, all the people, the nations, and the languages, fell down *and* worshipped the golden image that Nebuchadnezzar the king had set up. Wherefore at that time certain Chaldeans came near, and accused the Jews. They spake and said to the king Nebuchadnezzar, O king, live for ever. Thou, O king, hast made a decree, that every man that shall hear the sound of the cornet, flute, harp, sackbut, psaltery, and dulcimer, and all kinds of musick, shall fall down and worship the golden image: And whoso falleth not down and worshippeth, *that* he should be cast into the midst of a burning fiery furnace. There are certain Jews whom thou hast set over the affairs of the province of Babylon, Shadrach, Meshach, and Abednego; these men, O king, have not regarded thee: they serve not thy gods, nor worship the golden image which thou hast set up. Then Nebuchadnezzar in *his* rage and fury commanded to bring Shadrach, Meshach, and Abednego. Then they brought these men before the king. Nebuchadnezzar spake and said unto them, *Is it* true, O Shadrach, Meshach, and Abednego, do not ye serve my gods, nor worship the golden image which I have set up? Now if ye be ready that at what time ye hear the sound of the cornet, flute, harp, sackbut, psaltery, and dulcimer, and all kinds of musick, ye fall down and worship the image which I have made; *well:* but if ye worship not, ye shall be cast the same hour into the midst of a burning fiery furnace; and who *is* that God that shall deliver you out of my hands? Shadrach, Meshach, and Abednego, answered and said to the king, O Nebuchadnezzar, we *are* not careful to answer thee in this matter. If it be *so,* our God whom we serve is able to deliver us from the burning fiery furnace, and he will deliver *us* out of thine hand, O king. But if not, be it known unto thee, O king, that we will not serve thy gods, nor worship the golden image which thou hast set up.

Introduction

What is noise, something that makes a sound that gives sound that delivers a message? A sound that leads one to do something wrong or right, something that's heard or we hear with our ears, body or in our minds emotions or feelings.

There are all kinds of noise

1. Walk has a noise – Exodus 32:17
2. A cry has a noise – 1 Samuel 4:14
3. Every city has it's noise – 1 king's 1:41
4. the Lord can make you hear the noise that's not there – 2 Kings 7:6
5. The Lord said you will know them by their noise – Psalms 59:6
6. The Lord likes a joyful noise – Psalms 66:10, 81:1, 95:2, 98:4, 100:1
7. Even your hearts makes a noise – Jeremiah 4:19
8. Water has a noise – Ezekiel 1:24
9. The mind has a noise – acts 2:2
10. Something that is light as feathers has a noise – Ezekiel 1:24
11. But the best noise is this – Mark 2:1, Luke 1:65, Acts 2:6 to see and hear the works of the Lord
12. To hear that the Lord is with you – Joshua 6:27

Heavenly Nuggets for you!

I have a heart that was changed why –
1. I needed it
2. I desired better
3. I couldn't get out of it myself

1. Jesus had a plan before you or I knew it
2. Why Jesus gave you a purpose
3. Why- it must be walked out

Why- People or soul's are required at your hand. I the Lord gave them to you, before you were formed in your mother's womb, but you can only accomplish this with my heart. Amen

Jesus said that was Me

When- you were trapped, when –you didn't have it all, when – you couldn't see your way out, when-you called everybody and? When- mama and daddy did and couldn't

When - The job ran out on you, or you ran out on it.

When - And when some church people couldn't or wouldn't
When- You couldn't steal it anymore

I am so Glad you GAVE!

Who? ME A savior, and deliver, and a devil Defeater

Who? A life support system that never runs out, who never sleeps or is too busy

Who? Who cannot or never lie or die

Who? Who made everything for me I would ever need or want?

Who showed me the only right way? Jesus said I am the way, your truth and your life. Amen.

Ask the Right One, Watch Out for the Ball of Confusion

1. To		Get
2. Stay		Focused
3. Learn		Listen
4. Obey		Heart
5. Real		People
6. There		Confusion
7. Prayer		Much
8. Live		By
9. Choose		This
10. Your		Home

Simply the Word

ASK THE RIGHT ONE, ANSWERS

1. To – to get the only right answers
2. Stay focused on Jesus to stand
3. Listen, no nothing to learn
4. Obedience starts from the Heart
5. Real people have Jesus on the inside
6. There will always be confusion trying to get in
7. This walk takes much prayer and fasting
8. Men and women live by my word that comes forth out of my mouth, by whom I send it, you will know the truth. Mine is different
9. You will choose every this day whom you will serve
10. Do you really know where your home will be, heaven or hell, it starts NOW! Don't delay the devil's on your track, but so am I. I am greater.

Sign Here Jesus _____
Or the Devil_____

Simply the Word

Sections

You Need Jesus to Make the Whole

John 4:23-24 But the hour cometh, and now is, when the true worshippers shall worship the Father in spirit and in truth: for the Father seeketh such to worship him. God *is* a Spirit: and they that worship him must worship *him* in spirit and in truth.

Groups
Thinking?

Small Pieces
Thinking About
Salvation
For Fishes and Loaves
Or for what's in his
Blessed hands

In the Surrounding
Areas

Need
Salvation
Say it with
their mouths
But?
Their Hearts
Are as far as the
East is from the
West From Me says
the Lord

Which part are you
The – Problem or Promise

Will you suffer to Begin with Christ Jesus?

| Accepted Salvation | Part of | Connected to it to help it to Function His Right |

John 3:3 Jesus answered and said unto him, Verily, verily, I say unto thee, Except a man be born again, he cannot see the kingdom of God.

John 3:5-6 Jesus answered, Verily, verily, I say unto thee, Except a man be born of water and *of* the Spirit, he cannot enter into the kingdom of God. That which is born of the flesh is flesh; and that which is born of the Spirit is spirit.

Jesus is always pulling at your heart; He is always hoping you will come in with him, for real, not your way or play. However, to stay in his only way, to his eternal life of peace in his home made presence. That can never be denied or changed for any other purpose but his.

Sections comes from the word sect means outsiders or unbelievers or unbelieving believers will accept some parts or what they understand or what they went to school for, but not the school of kneeing down to Jesus in their hearts and minds and spirits. They still want to have some control in some areas of their lives, like before and it never works out, never, when they are in control of their own section or religious cult's man made to fail. Jesus said apart from me you could do nothing. Amen

Wanted Dead or Alive

Your saved or Jesus Saved

Still According to
Your fleshly Lust
In and out Acts 8:1-3

Living His Holy
Word Acts 8:4-8
Acts 8:9-17

Jesus is here

W-With
A-A
N-Need
T-TO
E-Eliminate
D-Death

Introduction
-Wanted_

Jesus said your living is not my living only, only your death is my living; it's Christ in you, your only Hope & Glory. To die for me is your only gain. Lose to gain all of me say's the Lord Jesus.

Acts 9:1-22 And Saul, yet breathing out threatenings and slaughter against the disciples of the Lord, went unto the high priest, And desired of him letters to Damascus to the synagogues, that if he found any of this way, whether they were men or women, he might bring them bound unto

Jerusalem. And as he journeyed, he came near Damascus: and suddenly there shined round about him a light from heaven: And he fell to the earth, and heard a voice saying unto him, Saul, Saul, why persecutest thou me? And he said, Who art thou, Lord? And the Lord said, I am Jesus whom thou persecutest: *it is* hard for thee to kick against the pricks. And he trembling and astonished said, Lord, what wilt thou have me to do? And the Lord *said* unto him, Arise, and go into the city, and it shall be told thee what thou must do. And the men which journeyed with him stood speechless, hearing a voice, but seeing no man. And Saul arose from the earth; and when his eyes were opened, he saw no man: but they led him by the hand, and brought *him* into Damascus. And he was three days without sight, and neither did eat nor drink. And there was a certain disciple at Damascus, named Ananias; and to him said the Lord in a vision, Ananias. And he said, Behold, I *am here,* Lord. And the Lord *said* unto him, Arise, and go into the street which is called Straight, and enquire in the house of Judas for *one* called Saul, of Tarsus: for, behold, he prayeth, And hath seen in a vision a man named Ananias coming in, and putting *his* hand on him, that he might receive his sight. Then Ananias answered, Lord, I have heard by many of this man, how much evil he hath done to thy saints at Jerusalem: And here he hath authority from the chief priests to bind all that call on thy name. But the Lord said unto him, Go thy way: for he is a chosen vessel unto me, to bear my name before the Gentiles, and kings, and the children of Israel: For I will shew him how great things he must suffer for my name's sake. And Ananias went his way, and entered into the house; and putting his hands on him said, Brother Saul, the Lord, *even* Jesus, that appeared unto thee in the way as thou camest, hath sent me, that thou mightest receive thy sight, and be filled with the Holy Ghost. And immediately there fell from his eyes as it had been scales: and he received sight forthwith, and arose, and was baptized. And when he had received meat, he was strengthened. Then was Saul certain days with the disciples which were at Damascus. And straightway he preached Christ in the synagogues, that he is the Son of God. But all that heard *him* were amazed, and said; Is not this he that destroyed them which called on this name in Jerusalem, and came hither for that intent, that he might bring them bound unto the chief priests? But Saul increased the more in strength, and confounded the Jews which dwelt at Damascus, proving that this is very Christ.

Your saved or Jesus saved

Jesus said you think you know me, because you know a little of my word, but without my holy spirit to give you life, you fleshly or letter knowing me is your death spiritually and then naturally, only I can

Give life and that more abundantly

Jesus said in me you have life

Jesus is saying if you know nothing, then I can fill you up with my something. I am the only one who knows everything. Learn how to stop listening to your own kind of spirits and learn how to listen to my life holy spirit. Amen

Havoc – means- Destruction, great confusion, disorder devastation. It comes to cause you to go astray from me say's the Lord.

Consenting –means- approval of what is done, to agree to, voluntary agreement by people to organize, given authority by the government.

Jesus said it means – Agreeing to do right or wrong

It's Time to Get God's Clean

Leviticus 12:1-4 And the LORD spake unto Moses, saying, Speak unto the children of Israel, saying, If a woman have conceived seed, and born a man child: then she shall be unclean seven days; according to the days of the separation for her infirmity shall she be unclean. And in the eighth day the flesh of his foreskin shall be circumcised. And she shall then continue in the blood of her purifying three and thirty days; she shall touch no hallowed thing, nor come into the sanctuary, until the days of her purifying be fulfilled.

Introduction

Jesus said my time is not like yours, Jesus said one day is as a thousand, and a thousand is as one day, Jesus said it takes my time and purifying plan for you, not your, your soap won't get you clean enough. It takes my Holy Spirit working from the inside out, to clean you up my right says the Lord. Amen

Purifying means – One who protects themselves from foreign or altered forms. To be free with deliverance from supernatural powers. One who preaches or practices a more rigorous or professionally purer moral code, than that which prevails. Jesus said it means – Be ye Holy for I am Holy Ask me for directions and then learn them (steps)

Purifying is on going forever until you reach Heaven or not.

Remember man can't make you pure – It takes Jesus on the inside of you.

Admit that Jesus is your only help, and then call upon him for-real for his right change

It starts with your heart mind, if it's not real, for real in your heart your mind won't let you do it. If it's just in your mind, most of the time you won't do it. God's Right. Your fleshly mind won't let you do it God's Right, obeying God starts in your heart before it's done in the natural. It's time to let he maketh me to be purifying and separate from this unholy world and it's God and serve them, and all of their tricks power, money and six is it's strongest drawing attraction and your love of them all, and they have you bound.

They are all right in God's right place for them and in his order, not yours your flesh wants everything it sees that turns you on right or wrong.

That's why we have to be born-again of Jesus spirit and learn and be trained to his word his will and his way. This is about being clean or unclean in God's eye. NOT YOURS. Amen

The Going Through for the Release Through

Introduction

There is one thing about when we change our partners from one to the other, from serving the devil to learning how to serve Jesus his right. Jesus said to look like him from the inside out, it's Christ in you, your only hope of serving his right, see your flesh dead, it wants everything it see's.

The going through for the release through Deuteronomy 8:1-20

There is a real good purpose for ours yours and my going through.

God has a real good or Godly purpose for our yours and my going through the main purpose for going through any yoke destroying battle is to get you out of you. In your flesh lies no good thing. You must learn to serve me more in my spirit and in my truth.

The next main reason for our yours and my going through is, to find out that, a part from Jesus as Lord over your life, you can do nothing, the next reason is, to help us grow and learn how to grow up into the man and woman of GOD that he purposed for us to be, before we came into this world, the next reason for us to go through is, to learn how to see, some are else need over ours. To see God's plan at a different insight, with his eye's and not ours, and remember

God is a spirit John 4:24. Your next purpose for going through is to, Tear down and build up, to help us to learn how to be strong in the Lord, and in the power of his might, not ours, ours will always run out and fail.

Jesus is from everlasting to everlasting and he can't lie or die, can you?

Basic

Romans 12:1-21 I beseech you therefore, brethren, by the mercies of God, that ye present your bodies a living sacrifice, holy, acceptable unto God, *which is* your reasonable service. And be not conformed to this world: but be ye transformed by the renewing of your mind, that ye may prove what *is* that good, and acceptable, and perfect, will of God. For I say, through the grace given unto me, to every man that is among you, not to think *of himself* more highly than he ought to think; but to think soberly, according as God hath dealt to every man the measure of faith. For as we have many members in one body, and all members have not the same office: So we, *being* many, are one body in Christ, and every one members one of another. Having then gifts differing according to the grace that is given to us, whether prophecy, *let us prophesy* according to the proportion of faith; Or ministry, *let us wait* on *our* ministering: or he that teacheth, on teaching; Or he that exhorteth, on exhortation: he that giveth, *let him do it* with simplicity; he that ruleth, with diligence; he that sheweth mercy, with cheerfulness. *Let* love be without dissimulation. Abhor that which is evil; cleave to that which is good. *Be* kindly affectioned one to another with brotherly love; in honour preferring one another; Not slothful in business; fervent in spirit; serving the Lord; Rejoicing in hope; patient in tribulation; continuing instant in prayer; Distributing to the necessity of saints; given to hospitality. Bless them which persecute you: bless, and curse not. Rejoice with them that do rejoice, and weep with them that weep. *Be* of the same mind one toward another. Mind not high things, but condescend to men of low estate. Be not wise in your own conceits. Recompense to no man evil for evil. Provide things honest in the sight of all men. If it be possible, as much as lieth in you, live peaceably with all men. Dearly beloved, avenge not yourselves, but *rather* give place unto wrath: for it is written, Vengeance *is* mine; I will repay, saith the Lord. Therefore if thine enemy hunger, feed him; if he thirst, give him drink: for in so doing thou shalt heap coals of fire on his head. Be not overcome of evil, but overcome evil with good.

B – Be
A – Acceptable
S – Saved
I – In
C – Christ

God's basic plan for us all!

1. Be ye Holy for I am Holy.
2. Be not conformed to this world, but be ye transformed by the renewing of your mind through the word of God.
3. Be ye reviewed by the spirit of your mind.
4. Be ye imitators of Christ.
5. Be strong in the Lord and in the power of his might his word.
6. Be not overtaken with evil, but overcome evil with God's Good.

Basic Revelation

Basic is something a lot of people have forgotten or left alone or just plain strayed away from, the basic or we could say God's set or present order system that was present from before the foundation of this world.

In God's basic plan of living, we have to be acceptable in his sight.

Not an anyway you want to do it plan of living. That's hogwash, that's like do do or dung, once it's out, it's out, will you eat it again through your mouth? Few people do, so once you get God's basic plan of life's right way of doing everything then don't put the sin back in your life again. Amen

Simply the Word

Who's Sinning Who?

2 Chronicles 25:1-4 Amaziah *was* twenty and five years old *when* he began to reign, and he reigned twenty and nine years in Jerusalem. And his mother's name *was* Jehoaddan of Jerusalem. And he did *that which was* right in the sight of the LORD, but not with a perfect heart. Now it came to pass, when the kingdom was established to him, that he slew his servants that had killed the king his father. But he slew not their children, but *did* as *it is* written in the law in the book of Moses, where the LORD commanded, saying, The fathers shall not die for the children, neither shall the children die for the fathers, but every man shall die for his own sin.

Romans 6:1-7 What shall we say then? Shall we continue in sin, that grace may abound? God forbid. How shall we, that are dead to sin, live any longer therein? Know ye not, that so many of us as were baptized into Jesus Christ were baptized into his death? Therefore we are buried with him by baptism into death: that like as Christ was raised up from the dead by the glory of the Father, even so we also should walk in newness of life. For if we have been planted together in the likeness of his death, we shall be also *in the likeness* of *his* resurrection: Knowing this, that our old man is crucified with *him,* that the body of sin might be destroyed, that henceforth we should not serve sin. For he that is dead is freed from sin.

Who's

The Bible say's that when sin is finished it brings forth your death James 1:14-15. ONE can-not sin for you, only with you or against you, and sometimes because of you.

The bible say's that we shouldn't cause our brother or sister to stumble.

There are two ways to sin.

IN Christ or out of Christ.

When you are in Christ, you shouldn't be practicing sin, because of Christ in you. It shouldn't have power over you anymore to take you to and fro, back and forth out of Christ. When sin has you in it's bondage, you're under it's power, if it wasn't for Jesus mercy you would be dead or die wrong, out of Christ. The bible says that all have sinned and come short of his glory. To let us know that there is non-perfect button, Jesus Christ.

Who's sinning who? Are you? Amen.

The Word of God

Nugget Time – Eat it, Ate it, Digest it

Whatever you digest, it will return whatever it is, whatever you eat or drink, read or look at or listen to, it always comes back up, one way or the other, from the top to the bottom from the inside out, you say you, you will or won't.

Are you doing right? Do you plan on doing it right? God's right. Question being asked, but are you answering it right? Your side, their side then, the real Jesus truth.

The Lord said my words are suppose to be your words, and your words are to be my word, and none of them will fall to the ground, they will accomplish what I put them in you to be send out to do. They will not return undone for I the Lord your God cannot lie or die. Can you? Amen

The Three Sides of Your Mouth

James 1:19 Wherefore, my beloved brethren, let every man be swift to hear, slow to speak, slow to wrath:

Proverbs 5:7 Hear me now therefore, O ye children, and depart not from the words of my mouth.

Proverbs 8:7 For my mouth shall speak truth; and wickedness *is* an abomination to my lips.

You lie not to one another speak 1 peter 2:12 or say faith out of Luke 7:6-7

Yes or No – Undecided?

Jesus said no one comes to me except that I draw them
Jesus said no one can serve two masters

James 1:12-18 Blessed *is* the man that endureth temptation: for when he is tried, he shall receive the crown of life, which the Lord hath promised to them that love him. Let no man say when he is tempted, I am tempted of God: for God cannot be tempted with evil, neither tempteth he any man: But every man is tempted, when he is drawn away of his own lust, and enticed. Then when lust hath conceived, it bringeth forth sin: and sin, when it is finished, bringeth forth death. Do not err, my beloved brethren. Every good gift and every perfect gift is from above, and cometh down from the Father of lights, with whom is no variableness, neither shadow of turning. Of his own will begat he us with the word of truth, that we should be a kind of firstfruits of his creatures.

James 1:20-25 For the wrath of man worketh not the righteousness of God. Wherefore lay apart all filthiness and superfluity of naughtiness, and receive with meekness the engrafted word, which is able to save your souls. But be ye doers of the word, and not hearers only, deceiving your own selves. For if any be a hearer of the word, and not a doer, he is like unto a man beholding his natural face in a glass: For he beholdeth himself, and goeth his way, and straightway forgetteth what manner of man he was. But whoso looketh into the perfect law of liberty, and continueth *therein,* he being not a forgetful hearer, but a doer of the work, this man shall be blessed in his deed.

Personal – Let the words of my mouth be acceptable in thy sight o' Lord.

God's mouth – but by every word that cometh forth out of my mouth, not always what you put in your own mouth.

Matthew 4:4 But he answered and said, It is written, Man shall not live by bread alone, but by every word that proceedeth out of the mouth of God.

His words will never fail, only if he is your Lord, your words are His words and none of them fell to the ground.

Different kinds of mouths

1. Good fruit mouth – Proverbs 12:14 – 13:2
2. Put away forward word mouth – Proverbs 4:24
3. Fools tell it all mouth – Proverbs 15:2
4. God's mouth – Proverbs 2:6, Matthew 4:4
5. Mouth made faith – Isaiah 29:13
6. Smoother mouth – Proverbs 5:3
7. Depart not mouth – Proverbs 5:7
8. Trapped mouth – Proverbs 6:2
9. Take heed mouth – Proverbs 7:24
10. The wise mouth to teach – Proverbs 16:32
11. Truth only mouth – Proverbs 8:7
12. Destruction mouth – Proverbs 18:7
13. Evil mouth – Proverbs 8:13
14. False mouth – Proverbs 10:6
15. Foolish mouth – Proverbs 10:14
16. Wicked mouth – Proverbs 10:32
17. upright mouth – Proverbs 12:6
18. A food can't open his mouth to speak wisdom – Proverbs 24:7

Jesus said seek me first for everything you need, not things that won't last or people who will walk away, sooner or later.

Simply the Word

Can You Prevail Over Me?

Ephesians 4:3-10 Endeavouring to keep the unity of the Spirit in the bond of peace. *There is* one body, and one Spirit, even as ye are called in one hope of your calling; One Lord, one faith, one baptism, One God and Father of all, who *is* above all, and through all, and in you all. But unto every one of us is given grace according to the measure of the gift of Christ. Wherefore he saith, When he ascended up on high, he led captivity captive, and gave gifts unto men. (Now that he ascended, what is it but that he also descended first into the lower parts of the earth? He that descended is the same also that ascended up far above all heavens, that he might fill all things.)

The Lord over it all – Colossians 1:12-17

I the Lord God created good and evil for my own purpose; I made the just and unjust to be rained upon, at my will. I called the harlot male and female for my purpose. I told the thief to steal no more. I told the liar to lie no more or you cannot stand in my sight.

I told the murderer to kill no more even with your mouth. I told the drunkard to drink Holy Ghost win. I told the sinner to go and sin no more. I told the single man and woman that it's no good to be alone, so I am making you a helpmeet, that's suitable and compatible for each other, I make it work my right, not yours. I the Lord told everyone to choose this everyday whom they will serve.

I told every one to work out their own soul salvation with fear and trembling, I told you all I created you all in my image, my own likeness, I told you all that apart from me you can do nothing, but most of one still trying to in vain. If I told your body not to move, it won't try me see it done.

Nuggets from Heaven to you!
Eat Good

Return service requested

The whole world is a stage and everybody plays apart, what and who's part are you playing? Tell the truth it hurts good or bad ha, ha,

Thought – I spoke it and it was done Jesus said if you just say it, then I will spray it, Jesus said you say it to them, then I will spray it through them with the holy ghost on the inside

Jesus is real!

How real will you let him be in your life? Walk He will he will.

Jesus said when I move then you move. How, where, when and with who?

He will, do what no other can or will do or know to do, his right.

The bigger they are, the harder they fell

I spoke it, and it was done, see it my way say's Jesus; I am your evidence, that you want to see.

He Jesus holds all hearts in his hand to turn it for you or not, to make them say yes or no, when he gets ready- they will have to move, it's open- he maketh me to lie down in green pastures, he leadeth me. He didn't ask he maketh it happen and last for his, his ever, can you?

The lost form

Before you knew me I the Lord of Lords the king of kings, the one and only true and living God, Jesus, transformed your last form, into my image form to be like me, my hold, your will run out.

Heaven and your earth will past away, but I will last forever, I am God I change not.

Simply the Word

Hooked, How Deep Is Your Hook?

Joshua 24:13-15 And I have given you a land for which ye did not labour, and cities which ye built not, and ye dwell in them; of the vineyards and oliveyards which ye planted not do ye eat. Now therefore fear the LORD, and serve him in sincerity and in truth: and put away the gods which your fathers served on the other side of the flood, and in Egypt; and serve ye the LORD. And if it seem evil unto you to serve the LORD, choose you this day whom ye will serve; whether the gods which your fathers served that *were* on the other side of the flood, or the gods of the Amorites, in whose land ye dwell: but as for me and my house, we will serve the LORD.

1 Corinthians 15:57-58 But thanks *be* to God, which giveth us the victory through our Lord Jesus Christ. Therefore, my beloved brethren, be ye stedfast, unmoveable, always abounding in the work of the Lord, forasmuch as ye know that your labour is not in vain in the Lord.

Hooked

1. In whom?
2. For what reason?
3. For how long?
4. Where do you expect to end up?
5. Are you sure it will hold for-ever?
6. What if it falls apart?

7. What if you can't put it back together anymore?

8. What if there is no human answer?

9. Then who will you turn to, as the world turns?

10. There has only and will be only one way out of everything that comes up to steal, kill and destroy you.

Jesus said I am the only way.

Jesus said hear my people, I am the holy one, and besides me there is no other God, that's real true holy, all knowing, everywhere at once, unseen, yet seen, the only God that knows the end from the beginning. The only God who will tell you truth only.

You have been hooked on everything and everybody else, try being hooked on Jesus once, for real, it will all change, you and your doing. Amen

Why, When, Who Jesus Fills It All

I have a heart that was changed why – I needed it- I desired better I couldn't get out of it myself.

Why – Jesus had a plan before you or I knew it – Jesus gave you a real purpose.

Why – It must be walked out

Why – People and souls are required at your hand, I the Lord gave them to you, before you were formed in your mother's womb, but you can only accomplish this with my new heart in you.

-   When –

-   Jesus said that was me –

-   When – Your were trapped

-   When – You didn't have it all

-   When – You couldn't see your way out

-   When – You called everybody and mama and daddy did and couldn't

- When – The job ran out on you, or you ran out on it. When – some church people couldn't or wouldn't

- When – You couldn't steal it anymore.

Who

I am soo Glad you gave!

Who – Me a savior and a deliver, a devil defeater
Who – A life support system that never runs out
Who – A God who can-not lie or die
Who – The one Jesus who made everything for me, I would ever need or want.
Who – The one and true God who came down and showed me the only right way.

Jesus said I am the way, the truth and the life, and the only light that can out shine your darkness, your hidden sin. I am the who that will reveal the who in you, to do the good I put in you for me. Amen.

Who is producing you?

Every spirit reproducing after it's own spirit

Genesis revealed by the holy spirit, Genesis 1:1-27

Genesis 1:1 – God knew already who was going to stay in heaven, and who would stay under the earth.

Genesis 1:2 – Then he divided his people of light from the devil's people of darkness

Genesis 1:3 – Then he called his people light and the other people darkness, because they have sin and love to serve it.

Genesis 1:4 – But God being God and loving, created a place for both of them, for a time to live in, and get it his right.

Genesis 1:5 – And God said let everything reproduce after it's own kind, light and darkness.

Genesis 1:6 – Let's divide the pure waters from the impure waters.

Genesis 1:7 – The Lord separated his people for and the evil ones from the beginning.

Genesis 1:8 – And God called his people heaven bound

Genesis 1:9 – God said I will have mercy on all, and give them a chance to be watered by me

Genesis 1:10 – There are more of us than there are of them. Open up your spiritual eyes and see out of mine.

Genesis 1:11 – Let everything be born-again of itself, like you must be born-again of me, my holy spirit to see and understanding me right.

Genesis 1:12 – God made everything to reproduce after it's own kind, who's kind are your? God's good or your bad?

Genesis 1:13 – God has a set time

Genesis 1:14 – God said my kind will always slow my light and my ways for a sign and for-ever.

Genesis 1:15 – Let my people by my example

Genesis 1:16 – Some of my lights will do greater works and some lesser, then there are those who just hang around.

Genesis 1:17 – Jesus said to much is given much is required by me. Not man.

Genesis 1:18 – Jesus said I have leaders of my light, and some that chose darkness, I created good and evil for my purpose, and all things work out for my good.

Genesis 1:19 – God's set time will come.

Genesis 1:20 – Jesus said let those who care full of my word bring forth more souls

Genesis 1:21 – Jesus said I will make your name great and take you higher, after me.

Genesis 1:22 – Jesus said I approved you and blessed you, and said reproduce after me naturally and spiritually.

Genesis 1:23 – God's set time is here

Genesis 1:24-27 – Jesus said let us make all these living creatures, after their own kind, but let's make man special after our own image, after our own likeness and give him dominion and rule over all of the other creation we made, don't forget he man will need a help meet, a woman, a wife of my covenant or my choice for the, to last my right made together by me.

Footnote

Not by the devil two men or two women, the devil is a liar and a deceiver too.

I the Lord made them male and female and put them together, what God has joined together, let not man or the government try to change my right standard of marriage. Holy standard mine. Amen.

Simply the Word

What's Your Favorite

Vote at Bible. Jesus. Holy. Heaven.

Trust in the Lord. He will never leave you or forsake you.

In all thy ways, see him first and he will direct thy path or your way to go, and who to go with. Holy – Be ye Holy for I am Holy

A standard – Is a rule or order or set order that you live by or operate by, already set in place before you got there or knew about it. To help lead you into doing right or wrong.

Word Helpers – Isaiah 59:18 He will fight for you – Lift up God Isaiah 62:10, Isaiah 49:20-22, - he will help. Numbers 1:52, Numbers 2:2-3, Numbers 2:10, Numbers 2:18, Numbers 2:25, Jeremiah 51:12 – My vengeance says the Lord. Jeremiah 4:6-7 Warning – God's anger against man's greatness Jeremiah 51:27 God's mercy how long Jeremiah 4:21-22

God's Standards – For – Real

Through God's word, we have a way to expose and identify sin and the standard for righteous living Jeremiah 50:2 – Fore-ever Holy

There is a way that seemeth right to man, but it's end is death hell and the grave. Forever.

Simply the Word